To the depths of the Ocean

Rod Theodorou

Heinemann
LIBRARY

First published in Great Britain by Heinemann Library,
Halley Court, Jordan Hill, Oxford OX2 8EJ
a division of Reed Educational and Professional Publishing Ltd.
Heinemann is a registered trademark of Reed Educational & Professional Publishing Ltd.

OXFORD MELBOURNE AUCKLAND
JOHANNESBURG BLANTYRE GABORONE
IBADAN PORTSMOUTH (NH) USA CHICAGO

Designed by **AMR**

Illustrated by Art Construction, Stephen Lings at Linden Artists and Darrell Warner at
Beehive Illustration.

Printed by Wing King Tong, in Hong Kong

04 03 02 01 00

10 9 8 7 6 5 4 3 2 1

ISBN 0 431 05561 0

British Library Cataloguing in Publication Data

Theodorou, Rod

To the depths of the ocean. – (Amazing journeys)

1.Marine ecology – Juvenile literature 2.Ocean –Juvenile

literature 3.Ocean bottom – Juvenile literature

I.Title

577.7

Acknowledgements

The Publishers would like to thank the
following for permission to reproduce
photographs:

BBC: Jeff Rotman p.16; NHPA: Norbert Wu,
p.10, p.21, p.23; Oxford Scientific Films: David
B Fleetman p.15, Doug Allan p.23, Gerard
Soury p.18, Howard Hall p.11, p.13, p.19,
Kathie Atkinson p.11, Ken Smith
Laboratory/Scripps p.25, Liz Bomford p.27,
Norbert Wu p.17, p.21, Paul Kay p.23, Peter
Parks p.13, p.20, Steve Early p.15; Science
Photo Library: NASA p.6, Peter Ryan/Scripps
p.24.

Cover photograph reproduced with
permission of Bruce Coleman Collection.

Every effort has been made to contact
copyright holders of any material reproduced
in this book. Any omissions will be rectified in
subsequent printings if notice is given to the
Publisher.

For more information about Heinemann
Library books, or to order, please telephone
+44 (0)1865 888066, or send a fax to
+44 (0)1865 314091. You can visit our
web site at www.heinemann.co.uk

Contents

Some words are shown in
bold letters, **like this**. You can
find out what these words mean by
looking in the Glossary

Introduction

You are about to go on an amazing journey. You are going to climb inside a **submersible**, an advanced mini-submarine, and be lowered off a ship into the swelling waters of the Pacific Ocean. Millions of animals live beneath the waves, each one specially adapted to survive in this hostile environment.

You will begin your journey amongst glittering silver **shoals** of fish, pursued by fast **lone** hunters. Then you are going to descend into the gloomy depths to view an amazing alien environment. You will see incredible creatures, huge **predators**, and witness animals unknown to science until very recently.

With the help of a submersible like this you are about to explore the depths of the mighty Pacific Ocean.

Viewed from space Earth looks like the 'blue planet'. Over 70 per cent of its surface is covered by seawater. These oceans are the most unexplored places on Earth. Most are over 4000 metres deep. Only the first 200 metres of this water is warm and lit by the sun. The rest is dark and cold, but not lifeless.

Some parts of the ocean are incredibly deep. America's Grand Canyon is a spectacular, deep land **gorge** over 1600 metres deep, but compare this to the deepest part of the Pacific Ocean (the Marianas Trench) which is nearly 11,000 metres deep! What kind of creatures could survive in these pitch-black, freezing depths?

The submersible's hatch is closing. You are about to find out.

The world's five oceans.

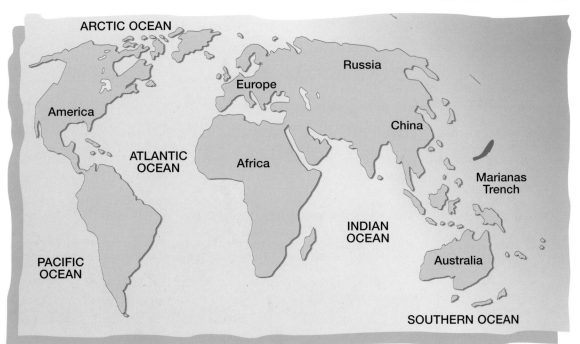

Journey map

Page 10

Page 12

near shore zone

Page 14

continental shelf

continental slope

Page 16

Here is a map of our undersea journey. You can see each part of the ocean has a name. We start in shallow waters and move away from the coast, going deeper as we go. This is called the sunlit zone. We will come to the edge of the **continental shelf** and drop down into the deep open ocean. The sunlight cannot shine deeper than about 200 metres. These gloomy waters are called the twilight zone. By the time we reach the 1000-metre mark it will be completely black outside the **porthole** window. We will need to turn our submersible's lights on to see any life as we sink further down towards the very bottom of the ocean.

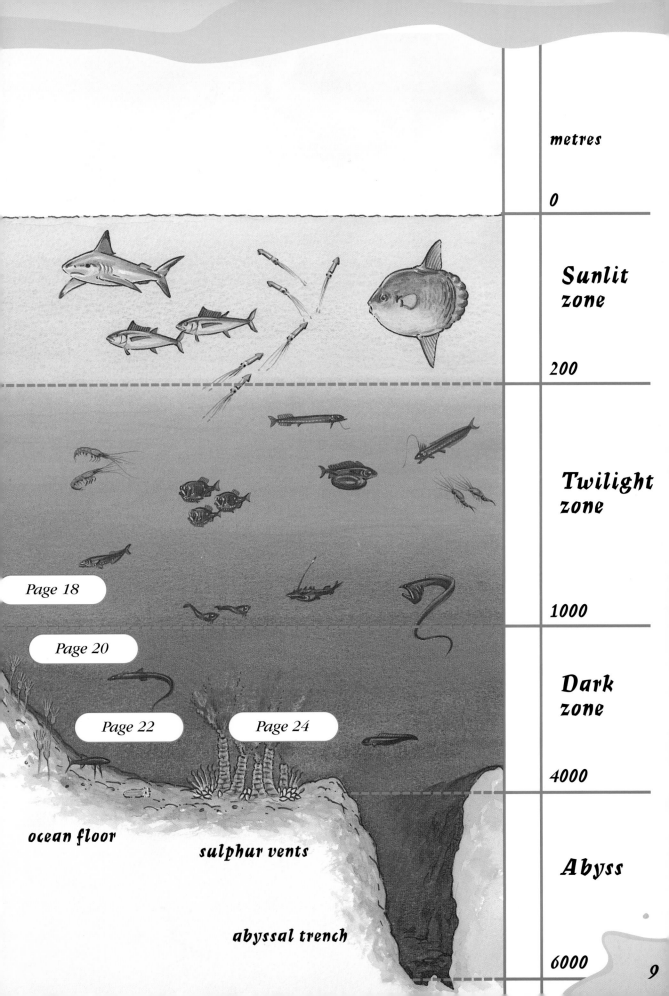

metres

0

Sunlit zone

200

Twilight zone

Page 18

Page 20

Page 22

Page 24

1000

Dark zone

4000

ocean floor

sulphur vents

Abyss

abyssal trench

6000

9

At the surface

As the **submersible** is lowered over the side of our ship we have one last look at the sky and waves. Gulls and a **lone** albatross soar overhead. Frightened by some undersea **predator**, we are lucky enough to see a huge manta ray leap out of the water. Tiny flying fish also break the surface and glide above the wave crests before disappearing again. With a loud thud the submersible smacks into the sea and in a burst of bubbles we sink beneath the surface. The dolphins that have been following our ship soon come to investigate. Bright sunlight glints off the silver fish that pass by in large **shoals**. There is life all around us.

The 'wings' of a huge manta ray break the surface of the water.

Portuguese man o'war →

This is actually a **colony** of smaller animals that live together. One is a large gas-filled float which sticks up above the surface and acts like a sail, moving the colony along. Others are stinging **tentacles** that catch food.

Sailfish

This fast hunter has a streamlined body built for speed. It can swim at an amazing 109 km per hour, faster than a cheetah can run!

Flying fish →

When a predator chases the flying fish it gathers speed and then jumps out of the water. It spreads out its large fins which act like wings, carrying the flying fish through the air for about 30 seconds.

The teeming shallows

Many of the fish we see in the sunlit zone are dark green-blue on the top and silver underneath. This makes it hard for them to be seen by **predators** from above (looking downwards at the green-blue depths) or below (looking up at the silvery surface).

Invisible to our eyes are millions of tiny **plankton**. In spring and summer they **bloom** in vast numbers. The plant-plankton grow in the warm sunlight, whilst the animal–plankton feed on them, and on other tiny food **particles** that are blown towards the ocean's surface by storms or undersea **currents**. Smaller fish feast on this plankton. Larger fish eat the smaller fish. Even giant whales eat the plankton, and other tiny shrimps called krill. Without the plankton most other ocean life would die.

1 ocean sunfish
2 skipjack tuna
3 manta ray
4 pacific sardine
5 common dolphin
6 blue shark
7 cod
8 dolphin fish
9 krill
10 pacific right whale
11 basking shark

The shallow water is lit up by the Sun's rays and is full of life.

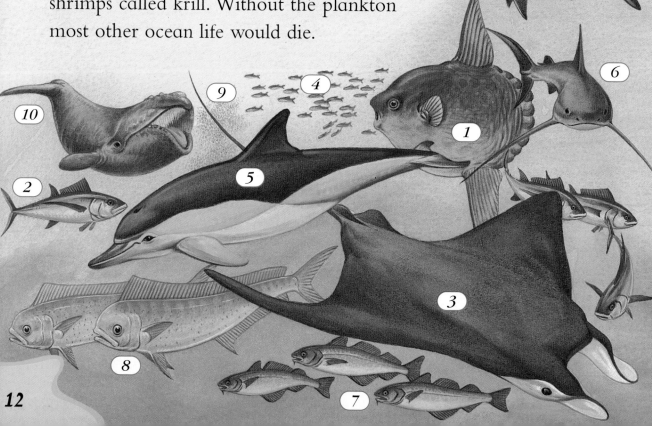

Plankton

Plankton are microscopic creatures. Some are tiny plants. Others are tiny animals that eat this plant-plankton. Some are fish **fry** or the tiny **larvae** of other sea animals.

Whale shark →

At 18m long this is the largest fish in the world. It is completely harmless and wanders the ocean alone, feeding on plankton.

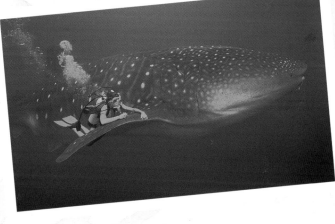

Pacific salmon

Salmon are born in freshwater streams and then **migrate** to the sea. They live in the ocean for several years before travelling huge distances back to the streams where they were born. Here they **spawn**, and then die.

The continental shelf

*T*he **submersible** dives deeper. We can't see the ocean surface any more, but the temperature **gauge** indicates the water is still warm (15 °C) and there is still a lot of light. We catch sight of the seabed below us. We are now at the **continental shelf**.

The submersible's whining **propeller** blades slow down for a while as we stop to enjoy the life around us. A green turtle flaps slowly by on its way to feed on turtle grass, a kind of seaweed. Before us we can see the end of the continental shelf. Soon we will have to go over that cliff-edge and descend down the steep continental slope into deeper, darker waters.

1 coral
2 sponges
3 seaweed
4 green turtle
5 barracuda
6 jellyfish
7 hammerhead shark
8 red snapper
9 california sea-lion
10 spotted eagle ray
11 pacific octopus
12 puffer fish
13 moray eel

The continental shelf marks the end of the shallows and the beginnings of deep water.

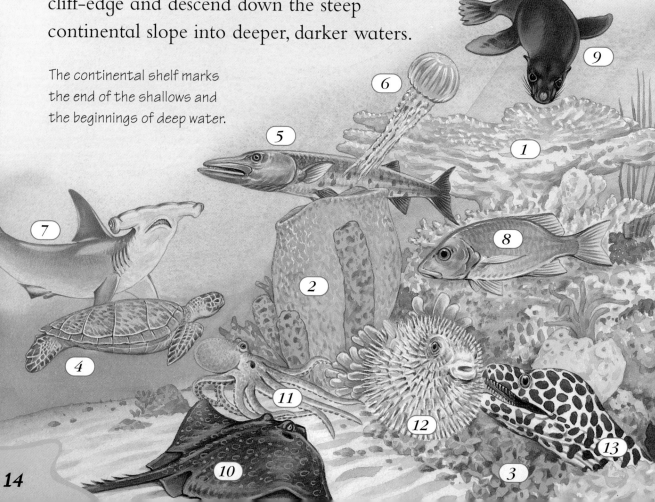

Blue spotted ray

Like most rays it spends much of its life on the seabed where it is hard for **predators** to spot. If attacked it can also defend itself with the two **venomous spines** in its tail.

Pacific lobster

This brightly coloured **scavenger** hides amongst rocks during the day. At night it comes out to feed on worms and other small animals.

Pacific octopus

This giant octopus can grow much bigger than a man! It can have up to a 9 m arm-span, but is a very shy and gentle animal. Its favourite foods are crabs and lobsters.

The twilight zone

As we dive deeper down the continental slope things start to change. It gets much colder – our temperature **gauge** drops to 5°C. We are so deep we can hardly see any sunlight, so we switch on the **submersible's** lights.

There are far fewer fish down here, but our lights soon attract them. The deeper we go the stranger the fish look. Many of the fish and shrimp here have what look like tiny headlights. They have special **organs** on their skin that produce light. These are used to identify and attract a **mate** or to attract **prey**. Some can 'turn on' these lights in a sudden flash of brilliance to confuse a **predator**.

These squid have large eyes and light organs to help them see and be seen.

Hatchet fish

Most hunters in the twilight zone look upward to see if they can spot the dark shadow of another fish against the dim light from above. Hatchet fish have light organs along their bellies and tails that make them glow just enough to match the light above them. Viewed from below the fish are almost invisible to predators. Like many fish in the twilight zone they swim upwards at night to feed in the richer, shallower waters when many predators are asleep.

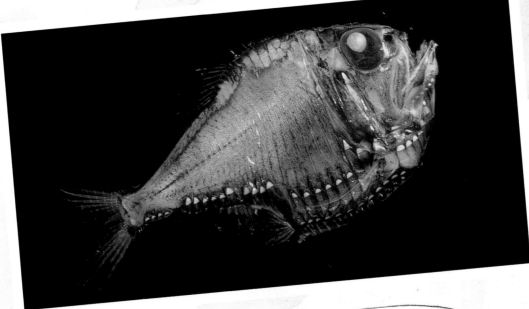

Viper fish ⟶

Like many twilight hunters these fish have huge jaws filled with large fangs and a special fin with a light on the end. This **lure** acts like a fishing rod, attracting smaller prey which the viper fish gobbles up.

Deep water giants

We have been travelling down for over two hours now. Below 200 metres there is so little light that no seaweed or plant life can grow. Therefore there is no **plankton** down here. The fish feed on animal **carcasses** or droppings, falling down from above, or on each other.

Suddenly we pick up something huge on our **radar**. It is two sperm whales, diving straight down into the depths to feed. We peer out of the **porthole**. These incredible whales are shaped like submarines and can dive to amazing depths to hunt for their favourite **prey**, giant squid.

Sperm whales have tiny eyes but can find their prey in the darkness using **sonar**.

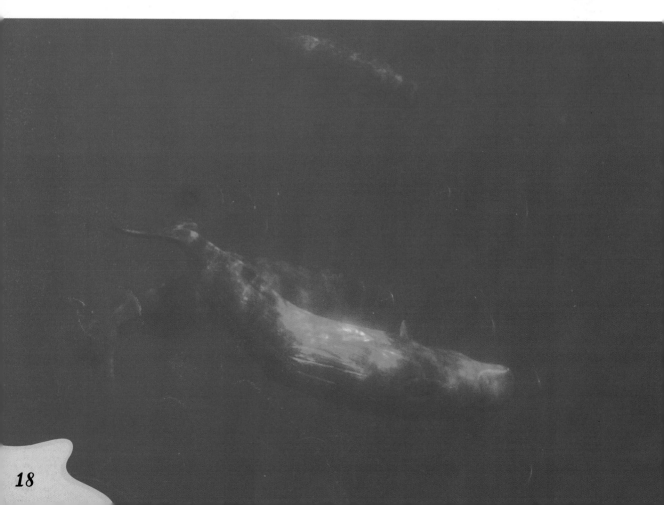

Whipnose

The whipnose uses its incredibly long **lure** to attract prey nearer and nearer to its hungry mouth.

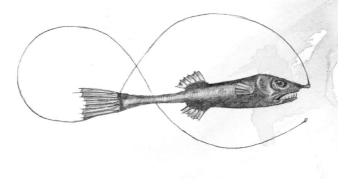

Sperm whale

The huge, blunt **snout** of the sperm whale acts like a heavy weight, helping it sink down quickly into the depths to hunt. The whale can hold its breath for over an hour!

Giant squid

These massive but mysterious animals can weigh over a tonne and may reach lengths of over 16m! The dead bodies of these gigantic creatures have been washed onto beaches, but they have never been filmed alive.

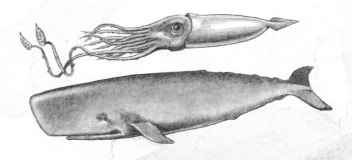

Into the darkness

We are very deep now – deeper than 1000 metres. The immense weight of the water above us presses down on the **titanium hull** of our **submersible**. This **pressure** would crush a diver like a paper cup. The water is nearly freezing, and there's no light. When we switch off the submersible's lights and look through the thick **plexiglass porthole** all we see is inky blackness. Down in this alien world many of the animals are completely blind. They are often coloured black, making them hard to see even with our lights back on. There is very little food down here. Hunters will attack and try to gobble up any fish they find, no matter what the size.

Many deep-sea fish, like this Dragon fish, have a long thread called a **lure** which they use like fishing rods to attract their **prey**.

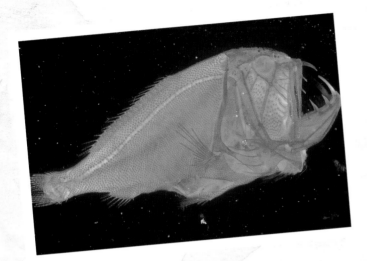

Fangtooth

The fangtooth's mouth bristles with huge teeth. It is also called an ogrefish – for obvious reasons!

Gulper eel ⟶

The gulper eel is like a giant swimming mouth. It drifts along until it meets another fish, then it opens its huge mouth and strikes.

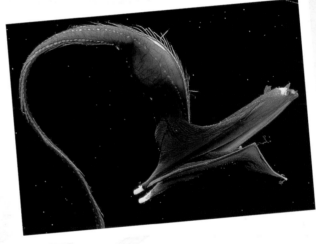

Deep-sea angler

The female angler fish grows up to 1m long but the male is tiny. The male spends its life holding onto the female. She has a lure tipped with a light organ and a huge bag-like stomach that means she can eat fish up to twice her own size!

At the ocean floor

We are nearly 3000 metres down now. The **hull** of the **submersible** creaks and groans under the enormous **pressure** above. The water outside is below freezing. Suddenly our lights pick up something below. It is the ocean floor.

The surface of the ocean floor is made up of the tiny skeletons and droppings of millions of animals. It forms a thick layer of mud that will stir up into a cloud if touched. There are no corals or clumps of seaweed. There are few signs of life here. It is like a desert. As we move along above the mud we start to see more and more snails and worms making their way slowly and carefully along the muddy ooze.

1 *deep-sea prawn*
2 *sea-cucumber*
3 *nudibranch*
4 *sea-urchin*
5 *sea-lilies*
6 *rat fish*
7 *halosaur*
8 *tripod fish*
9 *brittle star*

The deep-ocean floor is a still, barren desert.

Tripod fish →

The special fins of this fish help it to 'stand' above the ocean floor and wait to catch the **scent** of any food nearby.

Sea-spider

This strange blind creature is not a real spider. It walks along the muddy seabed on its long spindly legs, looking for worms to eat with its tube-like mouth.

Brittle star →

These delicate starfish feed on tiny food **particles** they find on the seabed. If an attacker bites off one of their arms they can grow another.

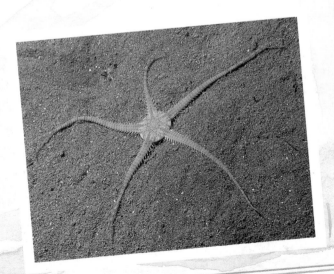

The sulphur vents

Suddenly our temperature **gauge** starts to show warmer water. How could this be? We start to notice more fish. Then we discover the reason. Deep below us water is being heated by hot **lava** and shooting up through cracks in the ocean floor. The water carries **minerals** through these cracks which form large **vents** on the seabed like chimneys. The water is also full of **sulphur**, which is eaten by bacteria. A whole **colony** of amazing animals live around these chimneys feeding on this bacteria.

Beyond us is another cliff-edge leading to a deep-water trench. Even we cannot go any deeper. It is time to return to the surface. Who knows what creatures remain to be discovered in this amazing and wonderful world?

Huge worms and clams feed on the sulphur bacteria. Fish, crabs, shrimp and thousands of anemones also live around the vents.

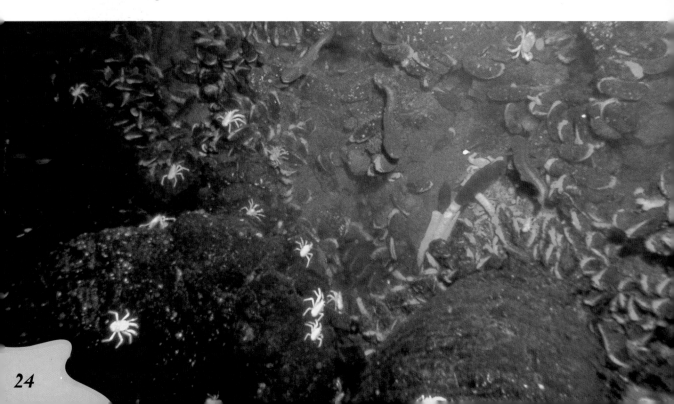

Tube worms

Huge red worms in long white tubes live around the chimneys. They grow up to 1m long.

A special world →

Until these vents were discovered it was thought that all life on the planet needed the Sun to survive. Plants cannot grow without sunlight. Without plants, every other life form would die. The amazing thing about the sulphur vents is the animals here do not need sunlight to keep them alive.

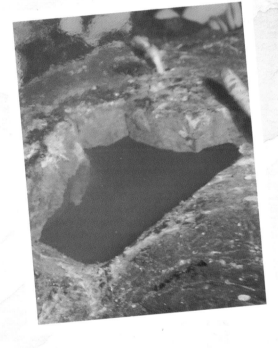

Giant clams

Giant 30 cm long white clams also live around the vents.

Conservation and the future

Pollution

For years people have treated the oceans like a huge sewer. It was thought that the seas were so big and so deep you could throw anything you want into them and it would be washed away. Sewage, rubbish and industrial waste like petroleum and insecticides were pumped or dumped straight into the sea. Recently scientists have realised that pollutants do enormous damage in the sea. Many chemicals get eaten by tiny sea creatures which are then eaten by fish – and finally by people!

Now many countries have laws to control and stop ocean pollution, but a huge amount of sea dumping still occurs.

Captains of oil tankers still dump huge amounts of unwanted oil into the sea killing thousands of sea birds.

Over-fishing

Many of the fish and whales in the sea have been hunted by humans almost to **extinction**. Modern fishing boats have **sonar** to find the fish and huge nets to catch whole shoals. Many larger animals like dolphins and sharks are also caught and killed in these nets by accident. Many countries are trying to control this over-fishing. Most whale-hunting has now been banned, but it may be too late for some species of whale, like the beluga, to survive.

One new idea is to create **marine**-protected areas where no one can pollute or kill the wildlife. These nature reserves are one of many ways we can preserve marine wildlife for the future.

The most famous marine-protected area is the Great Barrier Reef Marine Park in Australia.

Glossary

bloom	when something grows very fast and successfully
carcass	a dead body (usually of an animal)
colony	a group of similar things living together
continental shelf	the shallow area of seabed between the land and the depths of the water
current	a movement of water, sometimes caused by the tide
extinction	when a type of animal or plant dies out and will never live again
fry	young fish
gauge	an instrument for measuring or testing something
gorge	a very deep, steep valley cut into the ground by a river
hull	the frame of a boat or ship
larva	(more than one = larvae) an insect just after it is born
lava	hot, melting rock that comes out of cracks in the Earth
lone	only, or on its own
lure	something that lights up on a fish's head so it can attract prey
marine	to do with the sea
mate	when a male and a female come together to have babies
migrate	to move from one place to another, often to feed or mate
mineral	a natural substance, that usually comes from the ground, like salt
organ	a part of a body that does a job to make the body work
particle	a very small piece of something

plankton	tiny animal and plant life that floats or swims in water
plexiglass	very strong, see-through plastic
porthole	a window in the side of a ship
predator	an animal that hunts, kills and eats other animals
pressure	the weight of something pressing or being pressed
prey	animals that are eaten by predators
propeller	blade that turns quickly to help a vehicle move forward
radar	way of finding things using radio waves
scavenger	something that looks for and feeds on leftovers
scent	smell
shoal	a large group of the same type of fish
snout	an animal's nose
sonar	(SOund and NAvigation Ranging) a way of finding objects, especially underwater, using sound waves
spawn	when water animals lay many eggs together
spine	a special stiff or pointed fish fin
submersible	underwater craft used for deep-sea research
sulphur	a chemical element (also spelt sulfur)
tentacle	a long and flexible part of some animals that is used to feel and touch
titanium	a silver-grey, light but strong, metal
venomous	poisonous
vent	opening for gas or liquid to escape from

Further reading and addresses

Books

Coral Reef, Jump! Nature Book, Franklin Watts, 1991

Coral Reef, Look Closer series, Barbara Taylor, Dorling Kindersley, 1992

Fish, Animal Young series, Rod Theodorou, Heinemann Library, 1999

Inside a Coral Reef, Amazing Journeys series, Carole Telford and Rod Theodorou, Heinemann Library, 1998

Nature Cross-sections, Richard Orr, Dorling Kindersley, 1995

Ocean, Eyewitness Guides series, Miranda MacQuitty, Dorling Kindersley, 1995

Seas and Oceans, David Lambert and Anita McConnell, Orbis, 1985

Seas and Oceans, Habitats series, Ewan McLeish, Wayland, 1996

Shark and Dolphin, Spot the Difference series, Rod Theodorou and Carole Telford, Heinemann Library, 1996

The Atlantic Ocean, Seas and Oceans series, Julia Waterlow, Wayland, 1996